FOR WHAT IT'S WORTH
(A POETIC VIEW OF ...)

iUniverse books may be ordered through booksellers or by contacting:

iUniverse
1663 Liberty Drive
Bloomington, IN 47403
www.iuniverse.com
1-800-Authors (1-800-288-4677)

ISBN: 978-1-5320-4536-3 (sc)
ISBN: 978-1-5320-4537-0 (hc)
ISBN: 978-1-5320-4535-6 (e)

Library of Congress Control Number: 2018905449

Print information available on the last page.

iUniverse rev. date: 05/25/2018

Introduction

This book put itself together, literally. It is not just a collection of poetry but a following of itself, like a cycle, from here to there and back again. Almost all of the poems just came to me and I began writing them down, as fast as I could, and most often I could not keep up with the words entering my head. A number of them simply ended where they did because I could not write fast enough to put all the thoughts in my head down on the paper and could not remember the rest of the lines. Many of the titles of the poems were simply the last line. That happened when I was putting it all together to make it into a book and I realized I needed titles for these poems and so the last line of most of these poems simply became the titles, to me it made good enough sense at the time. At that point it simply fell into place.

When I decided to put these poems into book form I picked up the pile of poems I had on the floor and they were in basically the same order as they are now with a few exceptions. I probably rearranged a half a dozen or so of them at most. To me, 40+ years later, many are simply silly and in some ways a bit immature. And 40+ years later I figured I should finally publish the dang thing. But I do believe some are quite good and thoughtful and hopefully enjoyable. I can't take full credit for the poems because as I stated above they simply popped into my head. Perhaps the silly ones were to amuse me and keep me going. To me these were a gift. My hope is that this book has a few gifts for you. Thanks and enjoy.

Preface

This is a book to take a look at what you envision and how it relates to you and the world around you, above you, and below you. Enjoy the poems as individuals and how they relate in the order they are in.

The untitled poems that appear between the titled poems are simply notes of passing from one set of poems to the next, like a chapter break, or an interlude of what is to come. Thus you can consider the next set of poems to be the next chapter. Note: The second poem entitled "Foresight" is also the table of contents and a story in itself relative to the entire book and relative to the first poem titled "Foresight". So follow it as a story if you wish. To me that seems to be how the poems came together.

Foreword

Whatever we do in this life we do by choice. If this is where I'm at it is where I brought myself. To me this is a truth for all life. This is a book to be read as a book, from the first poem to the last. I believe one sort of follows another like a story, a story of repetitious time, and not just a collection of poems. To me life is time or time is life, however we choose to see it, just as everything we see, feel, or believe is. Remember it is always our choice. For what it's worth "For What It's Worth" is as I choose to see.

OR

What you believe to perceive
You'll receive

There are many roads in which to take
Take the one that is

For What

It's

Worth

(A Poetic View of ...)

By Me
Paul CN

'its'
whatever you want it to be
'me'
is a general term
as it should be
for now

as all moments in time pass
only to come again
as seen
as sight is within the beholder
what is that which beholds
anything

Foresight

I live forth to but an imagery of myself
    and should that imagery come true
it will all be new

For you and for me
    For the land and the sea
It's time we stop killing
    All that we see

From the earth that supports us
    To the air that we breathe
They provide for us all
    A place we can be

It all needs to be here
    Even that we can't see
Like the forces of nature
    That waters the trees

The balance is delicate
    From the air to sea
To the land that provides
    Good planting for seeds

Once anything is gone
    Never again will it be
So before it be gone
    Why not . . .
        Let it be

Foresight

Any way
life
a sight,
dream upon dreams
all rain's the same.
I stand alone?
      (I follow the path that leads me to home)
Sitting here in silence
the pathways parallel to greatness
I say what has it come
Love
the blind don't hurry
(w)hole or not its time
everybody does
change;
(parting words that have come)
hello
a day
Always
with you
little bird.
A few answers to why.
Hypocracy?
Meaning is to you
O'leary and the ocean
beauty is where you find it
pretty pretty butterfly,
to me to you
the campfire,
O' sweet reality;

justice
Mr. Frog,
she
then let it be written
by
the force
its cold outside,
silence
its raining
people
world,
who?
Memories.
Hey lonely
Itching,
the boob tube,
(truth) practical truth,
Hypocrites?
Yes
rock
the answer
yes someday.
Doctor doctor
to my home
it all comes back
together,
all you can do
its here
peace
children
any day
you?
to everything
simple
(or complex)
still
the greatest gift
symbolic of the cycle
of the endless dawn.

For what it's worth
is its worth to you
for what it's worth
is something new
but anything new
is obviously old
so for what its worth
its already been told

Any Way

I found myself
lost to me
oh tell me
what can I do
I look to here
I look to there
I see myself
filled with air
cast not a shadow
I see your face
I ask you with your grace
say me a prayer
filled with air
to float me
into the space
that fills the air
of everywhere
that we have been
and we shall be
and so I say to you
just be as thee.

Life

Let the rotten
smell of success
be forgotten
of all the rest
yet to be born
under the sun
from getting torn
while on the run
and fighting each other
while peace they smother
cause freedom is a word
that need not be heard
and time is the answer
the cure for cancer
let no one say different
it's all we have left
it is all that's inherent
that will outlive all the rest.

A Sight

Sitting here under a bridge
what do I see
Life
all around me
but I look straight ahead
I see structures
structures that burl so high
        of solid mass
that lasts and lasts.....

Yesterday was then
Tomorrow is when
Today we live in

Dream Upon Dreams

Inside looking out
its hard to see
without the aid
of all of me

Yet I climbed the mountain
so this I can tell
for all I found
was the bottom of the well

Dream upon dreams
did I make it that far
did I come up
to almost reach a star

My body was long
my peak was high
but he knew not
so we must die

My death is long
lasting my life
infinitely painful
by many a knife

I was cut
shaped by man
dispersed about
all over the land

Losing conscious
with my body and limbs
the road becomes long
the lights become dim

Printed and spiked
and crudely beaten
await the morticians
for me to be eaten

But alas the finish
is about to be done
I've been only prepared
for what is to come

My end is now
I know it is near
I feel it about me
I feel it right here

I see it coming
through civilized science
I'm being drowned
in their glaze of silence

Yet he cannot see
nor can he hear
but if you can
than have no fear

All Rains the Same

The rains fell
and I found myself
drenched to the bone
soaked with the pain they left behind
tormenting my mind
shading the sunshine
opening the gates of wine
leaving me without a dime
wasting all my time
cast out from the divine
can't read the writing on the signs
leaving my eyes in a bind
all I can find
I've been left behind

The rains fell
and I found myself
drenched to the bone
on the muddy paths that left me trailing
I'm ailing
must keep from failing
gotta stay away from that jailing
stay in when it's hailing
keep an eye on the railing
don't want to be trailing
better to be sailing
or living on a mayling
but like a carpenter always nailing
you left me trailing

The rains fell
and I found myself
drenched to the bone
and like the raindrops you left me crying
I feel like dying
gotta keep on trying
no time for sighing
just time for drying
want to be eyeing
anything I'm buying
no need for prying
I'll know if their lying
no strings attached for tying
and you left me crying

And the rains have fallen
I found myself

I Stand Alone

(I follow the path that leads me to home)

I walk through the crowd
they all stand there so proud
I see all the faces
life only in traces
they move as I progress
thus causing them much stress
so I settle down
but no ones on the ground
I speak to converse
and wait as they rehearse
they talk to their peak
but somehow never speak
I stand up real high
and look them in the eye
I shout look over here
come shed all your fear
learn how to give
you know how to live
but no one can see
their eyes are not free
I looked in their eyes
I found all the lies
as jealousy may be
remember you're free
understand what is hate
it is your only fate
come open your mind
to the treasures you'll find
it is in your lease
for you to have peace.

But no one does change
they all seem out of range
but could it be me
who simply can't see
or is there indifference
to a new inference?

Sitting Here In Silence

what do I hear
my thoughts
    where do they be as silence is around me
my thoughts are of solitude, onliness
found through quests of fate
     exchanged as luck through the wizard in my mind
       or into any fantasy or reality
         or dream of tomorrow
wherever it be
much has come to sight
    Though
Still this fate or whatever I chose
has come to being as a result of me
  and here it lays
Like a monument in my path
  growing with each breath
   is my tomorrow
growing with each breath
    is me
      today

"The Pathways Parallel to Greatness"

far from defeat
down the shady road of humanity
on the mat of time we wipe or feat
across the journeys of the aged wisemen
who seeth through the blinds of time
we ask not what we can hear
but of what we can find
and so we continue on
carrying with us every psalm
far across the desert of minds
taking all that we can find
till upon the oasis of palms we come
and find that all hands
touch one.

I Say What Has it Come

when love is lost
and all is gone
where do you stand
where is your hand
has your soul and heart been badly misused
where do you go from here to now
where from have you come
a world that is new and still undone?
do you find yourself searching your goals
like a changeling finding yesterdays coals
or is the shrill of the wind
screaming to come in
or is the rain beating outside
asking if you're going to hide
or stand up and fight for what is right
then you ask yourself why
would it not be simpler to die
for the decision of right or wrong
cannot be found in any song
and so you travel on
down the road again
wondering where . . . life will begin
and many streets and many signs
you'll see along the way
and some you'll find and some you'll stay
but you'll be travelling on
for your answers lie far beyond your goals
and only is it here that you'll find peace
but nowhere will past pain ever cease
as a tattoo it lives on as long as you do
but may it fade with age
then become only sage
from there may you go on to your eventual find
of knowing of the essence of time

for being is no more than seeing
all life you'll find along the way
in your search for a place to stay
and when you're at your journeys end
may you find a friend
 within

Love

life is much too hard
as often it is much too easy
I don't understand
      could you lend me your hand

I stand alone in a circle of friends
     I don't see any ends
   as there are none
I see only one
where am I
here is the reply
here do not many lie . . . even I

I don't understand
      could you lend me your hand

do your eyes see? Do mine?
do your ears hear?   Life
have you answers, have you questions
      I do
can you answer my questions
  I can yours, for me
  I don't understand
      could we take our hand

I love you . . . wherever . . . always

I understand
    let us join hands

When I see you again
I'll say hello
When I see you again
It will be the first time

The Blind Don't Hurry

Take your time relax
need not a decision instantly
    time makes up all minds
what is here today will be here tomorrow
perhaps in a different way, on a different day
    but just the same to stay
nothing leaves except that which is to be left
all only comes . . . forever
    good passes evil masses
    but all has the only classes
need not any glasses
                to see
    anything can.

(W)Hole or Not its Time

If there was a hole in time
what would leak out?
minutes, years, seconds, fifths, disease, tease
      (please see sight)
The whole is empty when it is full of ignorance
yet time passes continually
hole or not
fully whole and disabled a statement of fact
said not truer than stranger than it sounds
    (if you believe that the whole is there
     and that there is much to pass through the hole)
and what of the edges
why nothing of course
direction is everywhere
for limits are impossibilities, which are
                  contradictory to the whole
though in any field it finds its forest
for growth is basic of everything
        everything
leaving nothing to stop the hole
(though it is not going anywhere)
simply serving its purpose
as a porpoise has well done already
as for the birds the hole may not
    they fly through quite fast
though a tortoise has little more
    than elongated rigor mortis;
but such is life so he says
and the whole is tighter
but the walls are thinner now
   now – an infinity of time
              forever

eternity exists
in time
of understanding

Every Body Does

Traffic and sky
and clouds and why
all this has become
of mans first try

Streets and buildings
and pavement and cement
with light poles and signs
and who pays the rent

Airplanes and birds
and smog and pollution
rivers and streams
and fish and dilution

Construction and workers
machines and automation
medicine and science
for whos destination

Paced at speed
much faster than ours
slow movers are capped
and locked in jars

Wires and fires
and electrical steel
forests now wastelands
little fruit to peel

Mountains and trees
long and flowing
stripped and constructed
to keep things rolling

Economy and budgets
seldom work out
over and under
can't stop the gout

So what do we do
what do you suggest
its time we stop leaving it
to all the rest.

Change

Its raining, its raining
the old ways sustaining
But when the new is put to you
don't be too restraining

I know this chain
can twist your brain
and the weight
can be your fate
　　But look up
　　　　instead of down
　　and discard
that silly frown

Just relax and look your way
And you will see the light of day

I tell you now
its not all right
But that which ain't
will take to flight
　　And don't stop me
　　And don't stop him
　　And don't even think
　　of who's to win

Just let the sun shine in your eyes
And let it shine across the skies

And someday
you will see
all will live
　　peaceably.

(Parting Words that have Come)

When you walk on down
That long and dusty trail
My friend
You'll find the end

When you find the end my friend
Look at where its at
For every end there is a beginning
As for every birth there's death
And my friend that can only be
That which you choose to see

So my friend all that I can say
Is be alive today

Cause tomorrow

Is
Far
Away

Hello

So come gather round
Place your feet on the ground
Let yourself go
And never say no
Ceasing to run
We hold no gun
Helping your brother
Is helping each other
If we know how to live
Then we know how to give
Its as simple as that
So take off your hat
And open your soul
To let yourself show.

A Day

The sun came up
    upon the hill
It reached to the sky
    Just as a bird would fly

And so the morning rose
    Along with the day
For all of those
    Who have come this way

To those that see
    And those that hear
To those that be
    That have no fear

For each day
    will soon begin
And each day
    will soon end
And though the night
    May sometimes win
But still the day
    will come again

Always

No Memories
just new things
happening now
like the wind
as it blows
through and around me
so free
loose
settled
relaxed as a breeze
lifes little tease
blows through
my mind
reminding me
as I lay before
on the threshold
of all
of time
so settling
so comforting
is the wind
when it blows
and when it dies
for the wind
like always
is alive

No memories
just new things
happening now
in the trees
the wind blows
rustling leaves
as they tell

the stories they say
to me
to you
to look
their way
for in the sky
we may see
how high life
can really be
if we choose
take the road
lead us
too
be free

With You

I was just standing still in time
Searching for the answers
To questions I cannot find
And some help from you would be
    just divine

So if you're just standing there
And you think that you might care
My hopes and dreams I'd like to share
    with you

When yesterday left it became the past
Yet ordain me it did to grow this fast
As my erratum youth I've left behind
leaving me free to go and find
    tomorrow

So little was said it's on my head
If the sun could shine through you to me
Maybe then it could be when
    our eyes could see

The changing times we stand here now
So many fields we've yet to plow
Our seeds we planted life they know
And with them now I'd like
    if we could grow

Through the rains my love goes on
As in my heart the sun still shines
I wonder now if I'm right or wrong
In letting you pass with the times
    today

As a redwood grows it can also fall
Answer me now in heed of my call
And I will try to hear this time
In hopes that maybe we can find
    a better way

Now you've heard the song I tell
Caught the words just as they fell
I'll say them now in their way
This is all they have to say
    with you

        just divine
        with you
        tomorrow
        our eyes could see
        if we could grow
        today
        a better way
        with you

Little Bird

Sing us a song
of your highs and lows
telling us how
the forest grows

With your song
you sing no duty
just your part
of the forests beauty

And beauty it is
the song you bring
into our lives
whenever you sing

So sing some more
O pretty bird
so your beautiful voice
by all can be heard

And with its beauty
that it beholds
we have you yourself
to enlighten the roads

The animals who hear it
know things are fine
so sing out little bird
fill us with your wine

The bugs they chatter
the frogs they bellow
in tune to your song
in keeping life mellow

And all the forest sings
when you let out your song
in natures own harmony
of the rights and wrongs

So little bird
may your song never cease
and maybe someday
all will find peace.

Here I am at this incredible high
And I'll just stay here right now
With the world floating me past me

A Few Answers to Why

Why are you smiling
    cause I'm alive
Why are you crying
    cause I'm alive
Why do you love
    cause I'm alive
Why do you not seem to hate
    cause I am wise
Then why are you alive
    cause I am living
Why are you living
    cause there is life
Why then is there death
    cause there is birth
Then what is life
       everlasting

Hypocracy?

The word of the tongue
From the mouth of innocence

Meaning is to You

To myself I am a poet
to anyone else
be I am or am not
only is it their opinion

I can write anything I want
anyway that I want
I can make it rhyme
or give it a jaunt

I can say anything I want
anyway that I choose
I needn't punctuate nor capitalize
nor follow the language rules

I am totally free
you make of it what you want
the words are simple
they mean as they say

The lines are as they are
for their meaning is as it appears
to you or to anyone
throughout a millennium of years

For poetry is freedom
an art as all arts
not only of words and rhyme
but a coalition of time

From now to never
communication will endeavor
through thought or lever
contact will last forever

And so these words I speak
from the top of my peak
dribbling often like a creek
as some thoughts may leak
and sometimes sound meek
and may sometimes be weak
and some minds they will freak
and spoken all in greek
they should leave no one to seek
       the meaning
          they see

O'Leary and the Ocean

The ocean is a sea of fury
Of mighty strength and might
For tis the tale of O'Leary
Who challenged the sea to a fight

The ocean raged and poured its coal
And said I am the one
But O'Leary just laughed and said lets go
You've only just begun

So it started as a quiet calm
And then it grew and grew
The wind reached out with its mighty palm
And spread the waters astrew

O'Leary set sail in his skiff
Against the mighty sea
But when the winds began to shift
O'Leary could not see

The storm was mighty and fierce as Hell
The worst of all known time
The waves they crashed and swallowed each swell
Bringing fear to all mans minds

Still O'Leary he roared and sailed the waves
And said I've things to do
I've only one life to live today
And I'm going to live it through

But the fury of an angry sea
Is more than any man can take
As so it was for O'Leary to be
At the mercy of his own sake

A rock hit O'Leary's boat
It smashed it in the side
This time his skiff would not float
And O'Leary went down with the tide

The people they all searched and hoped
And looked for any sign
O'Leary was not a man to be roped
And he'd surely return in time

For ties O'Leary had often said
Were only meant to be undone
Rules he said would make a man dead
And send him on the run

Down at sea for O'Leary to be
Was not a likely thing
For if O'Leary you happened to see
You'd surely see a king

Though mother nature conquers all
And she spares no one
But O'Leary he would surely stall
And say its lots of fun

And so it was for many days
The storm went round and round
They searched all over the ocean waves
But O'Leary could not be found

Yet he was not a man to lose
Though few could ever have him
And he often said if he could ever choose
He'd do it all over again

Though this time he did not return
Somehow he had never left
He was just taking another turn
And catching a little rest

Yes in time of trouble or time of need
In laughter or in sorrow
O'Leary could always plant the seed
To keep growing towards tomorrow

His strength was less than few
His courage was above all
Anything old to him was new
For on O'Leary you could always call

Yes he was loved by many
And those who knew him well
Will tell you that he'd do for any
And surely be a match for hell

Oh I could tell of many tales
About this legendary man
But you'll always see his sails
All over the sea and land

So when the search came to an end
The people still could see
For never there ever was a friend
Like O'Leary to be smiling at sea

So when you mention the sea of fury
Everyone remembers the tale
That tis the tale of O'Leary
Who against the sea set a sail

Beauty is Where You Find It

Forests and trees
and everything green
but the colors I see
make everything gleam
in the air and everywhere
I see beauty at my feet
and in my head
and all about me
covering my bed
for I'm surrounded
in my beautiful mind
which took only me
to go and find

Pretty Pretty Butterfly

Fly me away
on your majestic wings
as they softly sway
and flutter about
gently flowing
with a breezy wind
that teases your stay
for it is in flight
you'll be today

Though your stay
may seem so short
your pleasure makes it lasting
as you live your life
in that very day
and beautify us
in every way
succeed in your goal
and find our purpose
fly on to ecstasy
inside of your soul
and to your destiny
as only you know
your life's complete
that very day

But while you're here
may we enjoy you
as forever is this day
glowing in your prime
forever in time
you fly about
throughout the forest
that gave you birth

and you return it
which such grace and poise
as only a butterfly
as beautiful as you
    can do.

For this moment
        Until the next in time
    Is what its all about

To Me To You

Its been a long road
and I been travelin' for a long time
         without you
         But now where are you

Well I been here an' I been there
and I'll probably go most everywhere
         but not without you
         Because to me you're always home

We look at this an' we look at that
I've got no tricks, ain't even got a hat
         but magic I see
         I see in life with you

Like the seasons always change
like the scenery when it rains
         the waters of time
         wash the past away

Yes yesterdays are gone
and we're only here today
         and perhaps tomorrow
         but always to stay

Life is like a rose
it just kinda comes and goes
         and it has thorns
         that stick in your side
            make your life
               blossom

So pretty flower may you bloom today
your seeds that have fallen may they find their way
and all that is here
may it always
smile on you

Like a seed laying naked and bare
like a yearling discovering its there
life begins
every day
everyway
everywhere.

The Campfire

Throwing its flames
all about us
   everywhere
it burns on and on
   as its beauty beholds none
for it is one . . . . . in the same
like the stars above
   six trillion none
all there . . . . . staring up
eyes in the sky
   watch child . . . . . you may see
   the stars, they see you
 no bigger than they
 existing as they
hi.

The flames curl and roll
            softly
  about the fuel
whirling and swirling
       and dancing in their delight
as they burn on and on
   till slowly they begin to melt
and smoke begins to fill the air . . . . . filling it
       to nowhere

The once bright flames now glow to embers
into the stars that lit up their eyes
but they too will sink
    not to be seen
 till night again

As night is day
    If right they say
A plight can't stay
    In starlights way

O' Sweet Reality

Come to me
wherever you are
from under a tree
wherever you be
from up in the sky
reeling so high
I see to listen
as I hear
the words you're saying
into my ear
sailing the ocean
from nowhere to there
they flow
in my mind
and everywhere
you be
I see

I think you stink
    But at least you smell
Oh thank heaven
    For giving us hell

Justice

Justice, justice, is justice ever done
        or is it all a game to play
Justice, justice, Oh tell me now what can you say
        if you are approached and asked to play

        Well you'd simply have to say
                I'll play your silly game
        Cause win or lose its all the same

Justice, justice, the social class that makes the laws
        simply don't want to see their flaws
Justice, justice, we've built a manned society
        upon the jewels of justice for all

        Still it is often said
                a mans worth lies within his head
        But in justice you'll often see 'how much for me'

Justice, justice, is justice ever done
        oh why do people make life such a game
Justice, justice, well the only justice in a game
        is you have to win or you lose

        But what of mother natures son
                who roams among the hills
        We've stripped her fields and fenced in his thrills

Justice, justice, it simply is another word
        still upon its call has fallen many herd
Justice, justice, Oh tell me now what would you say
        if you were approached and told to play

Well you simply couldn't say no
till you found that open road
Yes freedom is still a word . . . . . unheard

Justice, justice is justice ever done
well the only justice you'll ever do
is for you.

Mr. Frog

As I am walking down the street
It's funny the different people you meet
why the other day I met a frog
he was searching for his dog
Well I said Mr. Frog
I will help you find your dog
So he turned and he looked up at me
he riveted and croaked and he said we'll see
he turned his head and he looked both ways
"my dogs been gone for ninety days"
he said as he looked back at me
and proceeded to ask if I could see
"Don't think of me mean
just asking if you've seen
the changes about you here and now
nothing is sacred no fields to plow
Fences to the left building to the right
like squeezing the day right into the night
my ponds almost dry
my lily pads will die
and the muck I find below
is like the air the winds blow
My friend Mr. Toad he croaked on the road
and my friend Mrs. Robin
a worm sent her bobbin
and with all these new things
I've found nothing that it brings
So I really don't know
if my dog will ever show
So I just keep stopping
the people that are popping
down by the pond
past the water I am on
But most won't even listen

just think that I am missing
But those who come near
these words they might hear
And so as to you
my statement is through
and I hope that you heard
every last word"

Well Mr. Frog I listened to it all
never quite have I heard a frog talk so tall
But I surely must say
I'll remember this day
Cause it ain't all the time
a frog hands you a line
But I will remember just what you said
I'll let it settle inside of my head
And so till the next time
I hope you be fine
And oh Mr. Frog
I hope we find your dog.

She

There she stood and walked away
    from me it seemed like forever

In the raindrops she fell
like a cloud she swelled
like a stream she trickled away

    sorrowed plights on borrowed nights
    what has come has gone
        gone gone far away
            gone gone far away
        gone gone far far away from me

In the passing of time
I'm sure we'll find
some peace of mind
        for all
    all is 1 and 1 is all
      you need
    for two to make three
     easy to be
      simple to see
ask anything that you can see

There she was flying so high
that she is the sky
    screaming sand
      deafened lamb
    driving wind
      relating all her kin

Still the mountains may tumble
and the trees may fall
but she lives on for all
   all that survive
      these constant lies
   time to accept
      all is select

So she called in the wind
And she cried in the thunder
pouring life from her heart and soul
       still time plays its part
       from finish to start
       leaving judgement to be
           reality

And she's leaving me now
and I ask her how
could she not just stay
for one more day

Then Let it be Written

The land is destroyed
both far and near
the earth is torn
from ear to ear

Man has come
and man has gone
from the weary dusk
to the endless dawn

The land is bare
the fields are of rubble
the sky is red
from a sea of trouble

A planet of strength
and overwhelming power
although misused
has turned sour

The creatures that were
are not to be seen
for the planet itself
has been wiped clean

Of barren rock
from eye to eye
it stays this way
without a sigh

For the wind once blew
and now it is dead
the same with the planet
and so it is said.

By

Oh don't you wish
it could just slip by
I think it can
if we let it die

It seems to be here
with no apparent reason
it's obvious now
its past its season

I see no reason
in hanging on
once we let go
it will surely be gone

So you do see
it can be done
we need nothing more
to make us run

Once long ago
it may have been why
but we needn't it now
we'll get by.

The Force

I'm dying I'm dying
I know the reason
I cannot accept it
it has no season

It burns and it blisters
from deep inside;
a fire that is spreading
from within to my hide.
destroying and scaring
my mind and its will;
my power is withdrawn,
myself becoming nil.

Like the sun in my body
it rolls and it turns
scalding my organs
it scalds them and turns
to my stomach to throw
a flame for my feeling.
A flame within
a flame not healing.

The fire is spreading
to my legs and arms
to rot them and burn them
and destroy their charms
and leave them lifeless
and let them lay
dangling about
in a sanctimonious way.

Now that the body
has been duly burnt
the fire shall spread
to the mind that learnt.
to hate and destroy
to hurt and make sick
to love and make well
to build and make stick.
But this fire will burn
the mind and its control
to limit its capacity
of feelings very low.

The feeling of past
the feeling of future,
the feeling of life,
the feeling of death;
so much to offer
and so much to choose
so much to gain
and so much to lose.

This fire that burns,
burns only one way;
since in the beginning
to this very day.
it has carved out nature
and caused much strife;
we've based much upon it
including our life.

An extreme it seems
an extreme it shall be
and knowing all this
I still cannot see.

The burning inside
will continue to flame
and never again
will I be the same.

for fire destroys
and leaves only ash.
but this can also leave
an eternal rash.

But the mind has power
and the mind can be taught;
yet the fire still burns
so the mind will still rot.

A body consists of many things
As many things consist of a body

It's Cold Outside

It's cold outside old chap old chap
It's really very cold
And when I say it's cold outside old chap old chap
Do not think that I am just getting old
For when I say it's cold outside old chap
I mean I can feel that wind a blowing
And when with a wind it's cold outside old chap old chap
You can see the trees and flowers a rowing
But sometimes it is so cold outside old chap old chap
I say that I can feel that icy breeze
For when like this it is cold outside old chap
I can feel my body start to freeze
But it's so cold outside old chap old chap
Because there is a wind anew
This coldness I must say old chap
Is turning my flesh blue
And with the coldness like this old chap
Like the God of winters mighty roar
I mean that it's so cold outside old chap old chap
I may live for nevermore.

Silence

Its quiet
yes quiet
so quiet
its quiet

I listen
to hear
no sound
far or near
the sky
is still
at natures
own will

But its quiet
yes quiet

I look
to here
I look
to there
I see
no one
not one
see I

Still it is quiet
yes quiet
so quiet
its quiet

The branches
do not sway
the tree

it lay
the wind
has gone
it has played
deaths song

Yes it is quiet
so quiet
its quiet

There are no birds
to sing
no song
for this happening

Still it is quiet
yes quiet

Empty
is the street
emptied
from the heat

For its so quiet
yes quiet
just so quiet

For this street
plagued red
is now asleep
to stay
its dead

And now it is quiet

As death dies
    Birth lives
As night falls
    Till sun rise
In our eyes

Its Raining

The rain it comes
the rain it pours
life heals today
for scores of sores

The rain falls down
with all its decay
anything in its path
is washed away

The tiny ant, red and black
is washed form his home
while man is fleeing
away from his own

While the rain does not stop
and the water it flows
man does not stop
and his mind it grows

As the waters they flow
at a steady rate
it floods his ignorance
with an insatiable hate

But yet it goes on
and the drops still persist
flooding the pathway
of man to exist

The rain is stopping
man is dying
through stupidity and fears
he may drown in his tears.

People

It shone down through the sky of blue
yet not all could see
but it was there and it was true
God help them flee

The people stood and stared
in fright and panic
the warning as it blared
just made them frantic

They ran to here
they ran to there
if they tripped
nobody would care

Vehicles they swerved
then they crashed
but most just ran
as other were mashed

It was one for his own
and nobody for him
such are thoughts
such is so called sin

Suddenly it was quiet
the movement had stopped
the sky was clearing
the last had been dropped.

World

World here I am
World full of sin
World with your bomb
      you have done wrong
      push a button
      you become rotten
World there are bombs galore
World why don't you explore
World with its dictator
      have you found your peace hater
      and your totalitarian state
      is it so full of hate
      yet all want freedom
      why can't all handle this idiom
World you have color
      make no one duller
      when they cast their vote
      see their words are wrote
World though some people march
      do not work for meat or starch
      should you shame
      for all is not printed the same
      as in your society that holds back variety
      for when you demonstrate
      should you close the gate
World with its politics
World you've found your fix
World the bullets sail
      seldom does the assassin fail
      only your consideration
      will judge his destination
World are politics that great
      or is it money
      and how it rates

World listen to free speech
 though there are fools and people each
 like in your democracy
 that is supposed to be free
 I sometimes cannot see
 or could it just be a crutch
 ah but I say so much
 still world do not snear
 for I'll always be here
 never to leave and always come
Because world . . .
  I am Freedom

Who?

I'm going crazy
flipped out
blew my cool
ain't no more
as sane as you
don't talk
don't walk
just sit and stand
here and there
and everywhere
over here
far to there
in that chair
in this chair
at that wall
so tall
yet so bare
window here
opening there
outside it rains
everywhere chains
rust in water
wait for sun
then walk again
and shoot again
and loot again
play in rain
work in sun
can't demonstrate
our skills in rain
rusty gun
wet clothes
who would know
what nobody knows

no good man
works in misery
like rain
cliché, a miserable day
hang it up
till the sun shines through
and all can see you
when you're bold
no one need be told
and like a trick
you'll make it stick
while on the sly
the truth will fly
and once again you've fooled
no one to be pooled
so you see
once again I say
without a doubt
of catching gout
I wish I was
as sane as you
did not work
in rain or sun
too bad I'm so dumb
unlike you
good semi-airy-cons.

Memories

Memories that catch you sleeping in the dark
intrigue you and bind you blinding your spine
taking your mind through your soul
to memories of long ago

Facing you through the mirrors of your mask
catching the past and stopping today
as thoughts in time of passing reality
to memories of long ago

Like dreams in your sleep
in that unconscious state you find
that door in your mind that leads to time
to memories of long ago

Like shadows in the dark that can't be seen
a space you once knew, a place you've once been
and so the cycle continues to end
to memories of long ago

Hey Lonely

Where ya going
chasing a rainbow
won't get ya nowhere
to be found
so look around
its here
as someday
this lonely
will leave ya away
far away
to be free
in your mind
from Mr. Lonely
and his kind
though he'll find ya
wherever ya hide
you're smarter than he
cause he's lonely
and you needn't be
you're here
he's nowhere
anymore.

Itching

Got an itching in your soul
trying to tell you which way to go
pay it some mind and let it shine
on through to where you be
and you may see, you just may see
all the beauty that lay before thee
turn the corner or round the bend
it's always there waitin', to be found
as there it sets before your eyes
    like rainbows
        in the skies.

The Boob Tube

As I sit here weak an weary
At this hour of midnight dreary
I ponder over the reasons why
I should ever want to fly

Looking back and all around
I find I'm still on the ground
Wondering how high is up
From looking down

Sitting here dull an drab this way
I wonder what to do or say
For it is over till some more
Hark the boob tube nevermore

Looking outside my window
Sitting atop a thimble
Not a soul walks on the street
Maybe no one can find their feet

Gazing now at my stupid curtains
I find it hard to be certain
So I sit and stare at my door
Hark the boob tube nevermore

As this night fell very hard
I find I've gained three pounds of lard
Without a bite of any morsel
Gained it all above my torso.

Since the stations have signed off
I guess I may as well go aloft
Although I'll never know the answer to
The questions asked at the zoo.

But it's time to go to bed
Since my head is properly fed
For overeating will make it sore
So . . . . HARK THE BOOB TUBE nevermore.

(Truth) Practical Truth

Practical, practical
   factical, tactical
numbers and numers
   make numerous rumors
for seasons for reasons
   form useless treasons
democracy and hypocracy
   from bureaucracy to mockery
lame or tame
   its all the same
facts and fiction
   serve benediction
though all that we know
   would eventually show
if we knew what we knew
   Was actually true

Though it may seem
It was all a dream
Yet I still knew
That it was all true
Now I must go
I have enjoyed the show
My mind seemed gone
Yet time went on.

Hypocrites

I am many as I am none
I am a statue when I run
across the fields I call my name
across the grain is heard the same
So I speak and so I chatter
and so I find that's the matter
But if there is matter then there is not
is this so or have you forgot.
With some sight and the sense to see
tell me eyes what can this be
the fragrance of here or the odor of there
is this space or is this air.
If my hand were not a band
then where is it that I shall stand.
Is this that I know or is this not
is it only a little or is it a lot.
Speak my friend have you nothing to say
very well put in light of the day.
Answers and questions and opinions they form
accepted and rejected in order of the norm.
As riddles are formed this way and that
I find myself wondering where its at.
Ah but enough talk and words have been said
inflations and rations and nations are led.
A question is put to whoever to ask
is not a paradox alone a task?
So carry on I say form nowhere to there
I feel surely that you shall be here
                in time.

Your morality is your reality
Your understanding is life
Your wisdom is your guide
    Your time
        Is now

Yes

Throughout the stream of life
endless in the maze of time
we wander through passages of reality
   and down the isle of dream
inhaling the words of the wise
   shouting the words of the strong
   and leaving the words of the weak to die
Thus following the wisdom of the fates
   to our destiny
      wherever it lies.

Rock

Come look and see
what I have found
it is free
and it is round

I have found it
it belongs to me
no name upon it
mine it will be

It is called a rock
yet some call it a stone
I call it a bone
or even a clock

This rock I could take
if buoyant and large
and I could make
it into a barge

But if it were carved
like a diamond may be
and valuably large
I could travel a sea

Though it is tiny
small as my hand
dull or shiny
its part of the land

So I don't care
be it large or small
its here to share
    with all.

The Answer

And as the dawn came
And the sun shone upon the earth
Reaching into every crack and every crevice
Through the trees and upon the waters
on all the animals and all the birds
Thus all life began to rise
And this was beautiful
          To all eyes

All the birds in the trees were singing
all the animals on the ground were playing
While the humans just stood around
                  and kept on saying
       How can it be
      the animals they are so free
   why is it me   who can't see
     to find the key
And then the human began to think
causing his head to swell and shrink
so many questions ran through his head
he thought of himself as twice as dead
So with the swelling of his head
he decided to lie down and go to bed
only to find it was not there
and the fact about him that he was bare
with a flash of thought that he may run and hide
and perhaps the heavens would change the tide
But when he found he was alone
he realized the absence of his throne

without a john . . . . to go and sit on
having no one . . . . to shit on

So in conclusion from all the facts
he thought it his turn to get the axe
So facing the animals in much despair
he threw himself in front of them there

But as the animals kept moving about
he stuttered and stumbled and stood up to shout
causing the human such a sudden fear
he realized the animals they were so near

But they were there
just as he was there
Just as life amongst them filled the air
And with each breath they shared the air
And with each step they shared the earth
And with each moment they shared their birth
Within and without they are one in the same
As together they live and alone they're lame

Its all so beautiful the human thought as he stood
he looked about him and he felt the good
And with the life he breathed in with every breath
he felt his soul at ease and rest

But as his awareness grew much stronger
he somehow felt it couldn't last much longer
He knew too much only to know too little
And someday he said
          "I will answer this riddle"

So as the sun began to sink
And all the humans began to think
All the passing thoughts would take to flight
with the coming of the night
        Where will they run
            who may catch one
        Of what will it mean
            by whom its seen.

Yes Someday

In searching
my soul
I found my goal
wherever
I'll see
I'm here
always
how far and near
look
almost nowhere
listen
almost never
do
always
all comes together
simply
as people
confusing are they
confusing as me
only simple are people
like jumping
steeples
or anything
in life
complex
or simple
the only complexity in life
is the simplicity in life
before me
as someday
as others too
all sight
will be seen
all to know

will be known
in time
of its own
someday
if I believe
today
for music hears
all ears
in the lyrics of life
yes
someday

the reality you see
is the reality you be
for the dawn comes
forever

Doctor Doctor

I'm the doctor
the doctor of me
cause I know me
   better than you or he
                  ever will
cause I'm me
    ain't I.

To My Home

Hello house
How are you
I am fine
What can you do
I can do anything I want
      just like you
How do you do.

It All Comes Back

circles
circles in space I see
unrelated to time and reality
and here I sit with
with life swirling around me
where am I
and I gaze
and I gaze
and I gaze into the maze
I . . . I see
and the haze
and the haze
and the haze is gone
and all is gone
but nothing has left
and here I sit
and here I sit
and here I sit
for now.

Together

chatter chatter chatter
whoosh whoosh whoosh
down by the pond
life is coming on
in the trees
and all about me
I sees
life

ring ring ring
click click click
the noises you hear
awakens your ear
The bugs buzz
the air whispers
The sound of beauty
is all about you
openness is in the air
Yes the loneliness of the city
will leave you
in the company of the country
                    here.

All You Can Do

I finally came
to see insane
as wild as tame
it was the same
along the train
till my head went
in the direction it bent
leaving a dent
as it sent
Christ from lent
through the vent
that love meant
to the time he spent
driving the train
through the game
till he came to his find
that only in time
it would simply be
a matter to see
　　by all.

all is everything
as everything
exists everywhere
in time
and its happening
always

Its Here

Who will hear these words I write
who will understand
why do I write them
on and on
endless nights of endless lines
for what
where
I don't see
hope seems a dream
miracles a reality
yet I go on
why I ask
what is this loneliness
am I lost
am I here
where do I find an escape
is there one
answers that philosophize themselves
thus completing their own cycle
and then I wonder
more and more
I look on day after day
settling in deep thought
but what happens now
what do I say
what do I do
how do I find the answer?
    I understand.

love is
expecting nothing accepting everything
within and without ourselves
acceptance of our expectations
is Love

Peace

The morning comes
with its brightest sun
filling my body with warmth
my head loosens
as the sun soothes
for morning comes
a new tomorrow
for today.

The trees are crisp and green
and still waking up
settled and peaceful
as there they stand in their majestic beauty
awaiting the wind
to awaken them.

And so the wind blows
up and around these creatures of knowledge
rustling their leaves
swaying their branches
relating to them
the stories of the times
of where its been
and where its going

But the wind passes through
along with the new
and any old that happens to be
so stories are told
as told to we.

Yes with the morning comes many things
but also comes breakfast
and now that I've had my appetizer
and seen theirs
I shall feast
so till afternoon
    goodday.

Children

Let us speak
for we know we can
our feelings say
at a touch of our hand

Our children hear
with sound and sight
they see things as
no wrong or right

It is mostly you
that they can see
through our communication
they understand thee

So let us feel
our way through theirs
it is our life
and theirs
    we share.

Any Day

Today's the day
    for life to rise
shining eternally
    within our eyes

Though many hardships
    have come and gone
like winter becomes spring
    they too move on

As these days
    of sacrifice
like death they pass
    giving birth to life

For when Christ arose
    with life anew
he did it all
    just for you.

You

you are I
as I are he
as we are all together
you can be
whatever you do
or
you can do
whatever you be
as life is just
its all the same
to us

To Everything

It's always so nice to see you
it's great you're always here
you sometimes make me happy
and sometimes make me sad
yet most of all
you simply make me glad

Simple

Only time mutes the roar
from natures womb are we bore
when life we know
our self will show

(or complex)

And to thy father we hear
And to thy mother we be near
And to thy brother we see
And to thyself we be

Still

As everything must have its balance
so shall it be
for this may be something
but nothing is where its at
for now
as now is soon to become then
again

"The Greatest Gift"

The greatest gift we've been given
is time
The greatest gift we can give
is our self
The greatest gift from our self
is love
The gift from love
is peace

Symbolic of the Cycle
Of the Endless Dawn

Mornings come and mornings gone
day breaks the night aches
pains of darkness in tears of stone
eased by daylight in laughters home
till dusk befalls and sets upon
the joys of life given the dawn
and as darkness calls its mighty walls
wisdoms left to do its best.

For . . . a seeker of truth
as I may be
Yet . . . only do I seek
the truth of me

Printed in the United States
By Bookmasters